T0130366

VICTORY *Through* POETRY

Sheri Barrante

WestBow Press books may be ordered through booksellers or by contacting:

WestBow Press
A Division of Thomas Nelson & Zondervan
1663 Liberty Drive
Bloomington, IN 47403
www.westbowpress.com
1 (866) 928-1240

Poems and all paintings Created by Sheri Barrante

ISBN: 978-1-9736-6840-4 (sc)
ISBN: 978-1-9736-6841-1 (e)

Library of Congress Control Number: 2019909449

Print information available on the last page.

WestBow Press rev. date: 07/25/2019

Preface

Because of the Lord and His Greatness, I am writing this book. If it had not been for His Mighty Power, I would not have seen any more of the light of day. After fighting through a couple rounds of cancer and the medical treatments that were needed; finally I was declared cancer free. Believing and trusting the Lord Jesus Christ through the Cancer was where it all began, and now for around four to five years I have been declared and remained free of cancer. I am so thankful. And even more importantly, I want to reach out to the one that desires a word of encouragement, hope, and strength in whatever stage or journey a person is exploring, experiencing, or enduring.

Dedication

I dedicate this book to all that have prayed, encouraged and strengthened me through the years in so many innumerable ways. I also especially want to share appreciation for those that sacrificed, and those that gave in so many ways so I could stand while in the deep stages of cancer as well as after. Also, in honor of my mom, a special word goes to her for being a woman of great strength, charity, hope and love.

And for my father a word goes out for being such a hard worker and standing by my mom for more than 56 years in marriage.

Introduction

Thank God for a praying Grandmother. Around four years of age, I can still remember those prayers and love that my father's mother showed. She sent gifts across the states, and what I really remembered was the scripture tapes. I enjoyed listening to the scripture and cherished those boxes sent to my family from out of state, always knowing there was something special inside that would bring me a smile. One time my grandmother sent me a phonograph designed for children, and some fashionable clothes for that day and age. Years later in my early teenage years, grandmother spent a summer with my family. She stayed in my room, and she would play the violin, and always cook something homemade. When I walked in the house, entering in the foyer with the chandelier above, everything seemed large and magnificent. It was all I could do to find out what those delicious smells would be coming from perhaps the homemade pies, cakes, cookies, breads and meats that grandmother had made. After dinner, homework, and plenty of play, in the evening and every night grandmother would pray over me, and I am reminded that she had read the Holy Bible year after year all the way through.

Grandmother is no longer here, however, the prayers and Bible reading gave me memories I would never forget. With this impartation, all my life I have had a propensity to long for the things of God. I have been a normal person, have made mistakes but like many in the Bible, the important thing is coming back to Christ, being forgiven for sins, and moving forward in the daily new life Christ brings. This hope, mercy, and love of Christ has been so real. It has certainly helped me no matter what the situation.

This would become especially important when I experienced breast cancer. Every day seemed to be a new journey. It was hard to believe, I was too young, too busy, didn't have the money, yet and still cancer was still piercing and trying to steal everything that was mine including my life. Indeed, I lived life in measures, sometimes day by day and sometimes minute by second.

I would live through several surgeries, chemotherapy, radiation, and need time to heal. Everyday seemed to be a surprise, and cleaving to life was like taking medicine. I was determined that I would live life to the fullest, despite limitations, setbacks, struggles, and not seeing the end of the trial. I would not lean into the illness, but rather into the hope of the Lord. Every time I had a chemotherapy treatment, I would invite someone from the church to my home to pray with me to help fight and counter the effects of the cancer by going to God through many prayers. In addition, to the visitors I entertained, I was determined to go to church every week or a bible study, something as my way of staying connected to the Lord. Some weeks I was so weak, I could not sit up in the pew, so I would lie down on my furry coat that I loved, and listen to the sermon the best I could. Ministries were praying for me and giving words of encouragement. I would call them every week, sometimes every day. It seemed to help.

Fast forward, years later, here I am, looking back, I want again to share appreciation for all the good so many would bring and especially the Lord. I learned to live, love, and learn each day. And I could do nothing less to extend this encouragement and hope and strength through these poems. Each one is based on real life. Each has a gift of encouragement, hope and strength. And my hope is that you too will know no matter whatever stage of life you are in, you can live it to the fullest, find an experience in the Lord that will forever be your own.

Contents

PART I 1

- Just For You 2
- Miracles Revisited 5
- A Victory View 7
- Hallways with Symphony Sound 9
- Re-Image 10

PART II 11

- The Angel Came like a friend 13
- Not Night, Not Day 15
- A Royal Flare 16
- Fresh Joy 17
- Champion… the Game 19

- Reserves 20
- The Rush 21

PART III 23

- Lightning Bug Poem 24
- Lion Prowling 25
- Not Leave Him Out 26
- A Golden Nugget 27
- His Eyes are Aglaze 28

PART IV 29

- Beautiful Butterfly 31
- Royal Swans 33

Conclusion 35

PART I

Just For You

Here is a Word, A Heart on a Piece of Paper
For You
Can you hear His love that has raced through Eternity to meet you
His Love
Now, right now on purpose
If wondering in the Light of this Day
This is for you
Hope, a Friend, a Special Word
It is all for you
Only you were on my mind
If having been ill, had surgeries, another says me too
Nevertheless, you are special before, now and After,
And Hope Still Never fails
You may have to see your beauty a new way
But you are Beautiful and the Creator of the Universe loves you
And I love you, and this book was and is and always will be for you
The way you would love yourself and the way you will love yourself
You are Beautiful
Hold up your head, you are now recruited
To know you are special
This poem and book was written just for you.

About the poem, "For You". When I thought of writing this book there was this battle on the inside going on. Should I put my feelings on paper for the world to see? I am hidden and feel somewhat secure in my little world. But my heart knew, it just knew, that I wanted to make a positive difference and share beyond my private little world. I wanted to reach someone and really encourage and let someone know how special they are, you are, no matter what. No matter what the doctor reports may say, no matter the shocking news you may have heard, or even if you have been walking through life just kind of bored and uninspired, there is more. You need to know there is so much more.

You may be about to experience an ocean breeze with the smell of salt water like you never have before. Perhaps a flower near you brings you a memory of a special occasion that brings you a smile. Or maybe the more is just a moment to kick up your feet. Whatever it may be for you, there is still a something more, I encourage you to let the idea embrace you and move forward.

Barrante

Miracles Revisited

It was about four to five years ago
At the beginning
When a surprise suddenly tried to have me
Always reminded that Christ
Never left
The Winds of Eternity
Visited and Revisited
Reminded never alone
Sight was no comparison for the love He showed
Doctors came assuring
Yet these plans, schedules
My time would not be my own
Chemotherapy, surgeries
Approaching the alters like never before
Yet His Mighty Hand and Eyes
His Hold, His Strength, He Amazed
Through friends and prayers
Miracles would visit
Also there were Angels sent,
Spaces of Time, Christ had never died,
He was alive
I knew, He was everywhere
Nowhere did I hide.

Miracle reflection: When I was in the depth of the walk of fighting cancer, no matter how I would feel, days I could not get out of the bed, or days I wanted to be around someone besides my cat, I came to realize the Lord was with me, and He is also always with you. You may not have bouts with cancer, nevertheless, He is still with you, He is not leaving you. You do not have to be your best, nor your worst. He accepts you. He loves you just as you are.

A Victory View

A Victory View
With Crystalline Reflections
In summer Sun so Bright
Coloring my life
In a Brief Span of Time
Where Victory and I met.

About Victory: Victory over a trial does not occur without the trial. It is the trial where we see ourselves and realize and interact with ourselves in a way we otherwise would not. It is in this place where we can meet small, medium, and large victories. It is here where we muster the all within to tackle the challenging. It is in this place where victory and a person will meet.

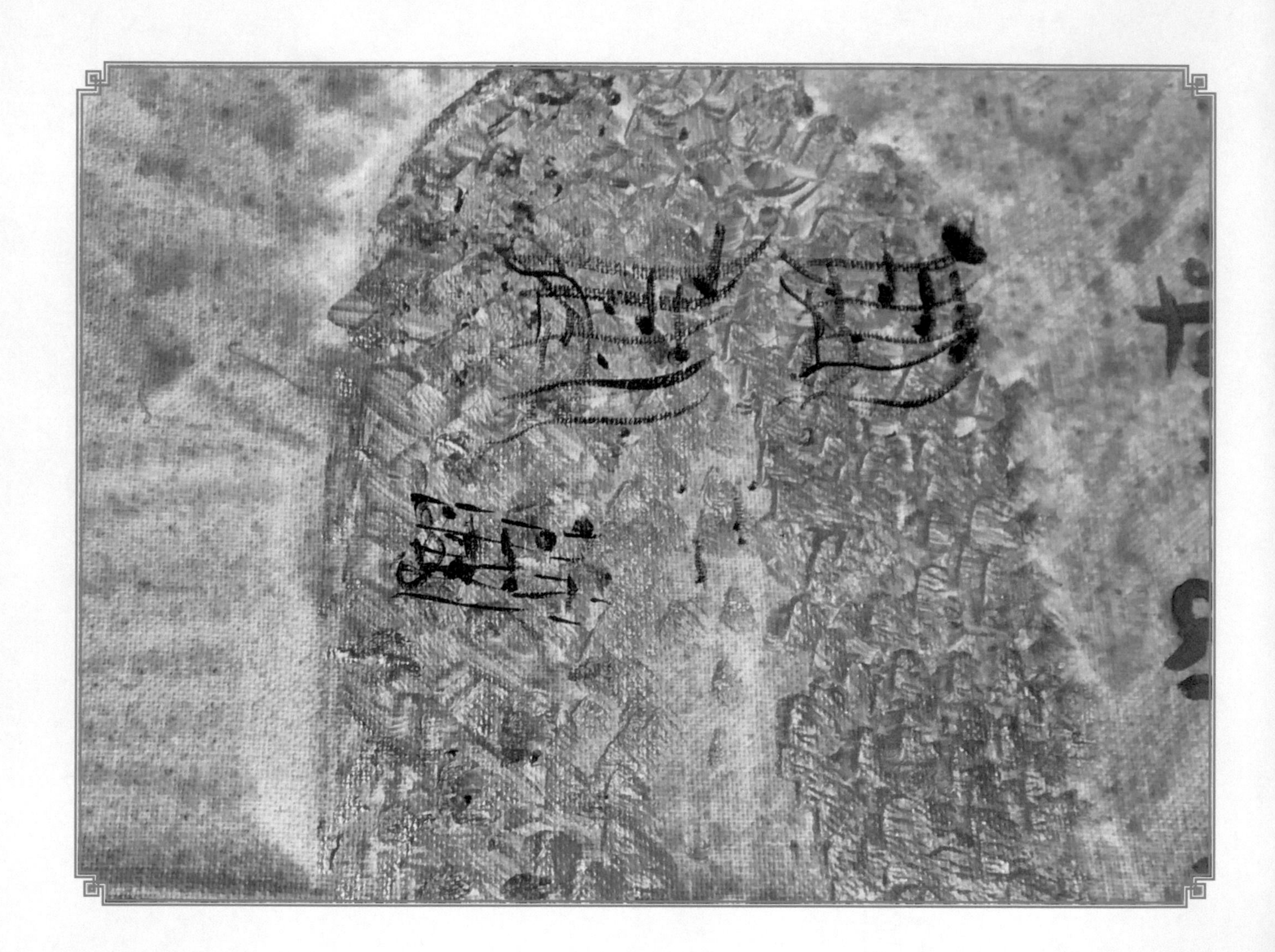

Hallways with Symphony Sound

Walking through Hallways
In a Symphony Journey
Wedding Bells Had Wrung
Years Gone by
Where there are smile Creases
To show for everyone, and Yet so
Somewhere the Babes in Cribs Grow
While Yet Hallways of Time Are Revisited through a Song.

A time note: Isn't it so true that a song can take us to those places in life, those reflections that surpass time? It does seem that songs can be timeless.

Re-Image

Imagine an image that you never dreamed was your own.
Like no other, with no plans
And yet it would become you
You never asked for this, You never imagined this
Rounding off, with an exclamation point!
A Re-Image
Softly seeing yourself, and
Remembering
Contemplating
Embracing
Changing.

Image reflections: This poem was meant to encourage anyone who is experiencing a change whether it be about life in general or in your physical body. Change is not always instant. We do not always process it suddenly. And however much time it takes it is okay. Whether you contemplate your change slowly right then, or years later it is ok. If you must reflect and then accept, or perhaps not to accept but to be at peace with yourself nevertheless. You are special and being merciful towards yourself is all okay.

PART II

The Angel Came like a friend

The Angel Came like a friend
Full of Encouragement, Hope and Strength
In the Shape of a Man
Its Skin Was Flawless
Never Saw Him again,
Its message was a flaming Fire
That Burned within
It was a message the Savior would give
I'm so pleased
Don't ever stop fighting
Don't give in.

Reflection: For some of you, you may meet someone who is so kind to you, you call them an angel. For others, you actually have had a super experience with one that you have no choice but to call it an angel. For me, when the Lord knew I needed encouragement and strength and some joy while struggling to accept the side effects of chemotherapy; It was like a treasure, meeting what I can only describe as an angel. I hope I will never forget how encouraging this was. I certainly never had the intention at that time to encourage myself in this way. However, the visiting angel was effective, and I realized that the Lord was sending me His encouragement in this special way. I never saw the angel enter or exit through the door of the store I was in, nor did I ever see it buy anything. It did have a physical body, and was as solid as the desk I am now working on. One never knows the wonderful things God has for those He calls His own. Have you also been visited by an angel? Perhaps while unaware of it, only to realize later that something very special had happened?

Not Night, Not Day

A Place I could not describe
The light was so bright
One that was a King
With the children
He ministered yet to me
He was love, peace, Patience
So Kind, Caring
His appearance
All I could see
Power in and out of His Robe
His Royal Sash it flowed
He Was All I need.

Royal thoughts: The Lord is merciful and His children know Him. He does visit in many different ways. This particular poem was my experience a couple of times, where it did seem I encountered the Lord in a special way. Just ask, if you desire a visit with the Lord, let Him know. How will you ever know if you do not ask?

A Royal Flare

Engaged in a War
In the Night
With Allies Still I stood
The King got wind of it
Through many prayers
His Royal Blood;
It flowed,
Through my veins
It was unsurmountable
Yet I knew, things were better
I had taken ground, air and byways
It was surety
The King had conquered everything.

This poem is a reflection of the warfare discussed in Ephesians, Daniel and many other Books of the Bible. It also alludes to the powerful Blood of Jesus/Yeshua, and how the Lord is our Conquering King. We can trust the Lord. We can trust He is never afraid. He does conquer, and we can be encouraged that no matter what He is with us. Have you had a time, that otherwise, you know would not have turned out alright, but in the end it did? You just knew that God had been with you and was for you through and through?

Fresh Joy

Freshly
Light Rain
Where lie reserves of Glory
Sprinkled in the Hour
You will grow strong here
Joy comes near
Your strength is as a fortified city
Slowly freedom is all about me.

A Joy Note: This poem alludes to a place or time where one is reminded of the joy, the refreshment and the strength that sets us free when we soak and refresh ourselves in the Lords' glory. Basking in the Lord also helps bring healing, the kind of healing we really need, that helps build the immune system and pushes one towards a higher level of care. Have you experienced this as well?

Sheri Barrant

Champion... the Game

I would have this Game
It would not have me.
Elements were chosen for me,
Yet this would be my game.
They called it cancer
For some it was crying for months and staying in bed,
For others it was shying away from family and all called a friend.
For yet others, it was a chance at a new thing.
A chance to overcome and never let it have them.
For me it was cancer with a small c.
It does not matter the they…
They would say don't plan, don't try, relax, rest, let it be a Cancer with a capital C.
Determined Strategic, this would not be the game.
No....with Jesus Christ the King…
With Encouragement…with all the Lord would bring
The Name of the Game would be to have my mind on thoughts of Above,
Studying, Leaning, Learning, and to love
Reaching out, giving good, planning with strategy with one from above,
The Game was Eventful
It was life,
It chose the element, But it was my game, with my choices, and
I never succumbed.

Champion Reflections: Can you see yourself reaching out to find Christ? This was my experience, while taking a Master's Degree and plowing through the stages of Cancer treatment at the same time. The struggle in life did come, yet with Christ freedom was found. Coming through with victory, I would determine to write this book. Perhaps you have found a difficulty or two, the hard and unexpected, this is where you can see it through. Rising above it, may come forth in many ways. It may be to encourage someone else. And yet it also may be to embrace the positive and make a change. It is all a choice you can make, when you do, you are taking the journey on like a champion, and making it a victorious game.

Reserves

Is there anything that Ails you
Dig in, Deeper now
To the Greater Reserve
There is a place of healing
So much greater,
Where Jesus is King
And He reigns there.

A Note about Reserves: The time to come closer to the Lord is right where you are. It could be a tough place or a happy and satisfying place. It is not just the good days that are okay to press into the Lord but also the difficult ones. The Lord is our Healer, and Redeemer. He wants us close to Him, to know all about our concerns because He truly does care.

The Rush

Do you feel like a Rush
A Wind
Running through Life
Always in a Hurry
Never Satisfied
The grip and fear, If only's and Maybe's
Truth is you confidently can, and will, one steady decision at a time
All coming together
This is your stride
Fact is, Truly it is your life.

Stride: If you have received a lurking report, and the questions are racing through your mind, know that you can get through this, one decision at a time. You don't have to make every decision all at once. When I went through cancer this is what I did, took life one decision at a time. Knowing you can take whatever it is in your stride. Looking back after all yes it is your life.

PART III

Lightning Bug Poem

It could be dawn, it could be day
Whatever the clock may say
It is a hope and dream to catch
Like a lightening bug in plain sight
To be grasped
To let go
For the next one to be seen
Before it is gone
No need to look back
Just to be here in the now.
Absorb it, enjoy it,
This moment is right in plain sight.

Now moments: Is there something special that you like, something special you can apply? Don't be afraid to try, the fact that you can see it, might be the key right there. What have you experienced or what would you like to experience that is special and could make a keepsake memory?

Lion Prowling

Prowling
Roaming
Setting the Stage
Of the Tribe of Judah
Powerful, Mighty
The All that shall
He is Conquering,
Delivering
To any that should Call His Name

The Challenge Question: Do we dare to call His Name and find out even if it is over time, how He is moving about in our lives, in small and big things? Can we see how powerful He is, and amazing? This poem is not only an encouragement but also a challenge.

Not Leave Him Out

Jesus, I would not leave Him out
Any more than a key that opens the front door
Where you beckon from the heat of the day
Racing, your heart,
Draws ever nigh,
The world pivots on His existence
Consistently He invites
Stepping more closely
You will certainly see
If you knock
He will set you free.

A Pivot: To enter your home, you must have the key. Daily you remember your key to enter in; comparably so it is also crucial that each day one invites the Lord to enter the day and experience life in a greater way. The Lord is there for anyone who calls His Name. To master fear of what could be, to allow Him into your life in the small and large ways. He really does care. He is there.

A Golden Nugget

A Golden Nugget
In a Re Fined fire
More Beautiful than before
Great things and greater
For those that wait on the Lord
Place your energies here,
Look back
See your better
Look forward
See the Firey Hope.

Hope Reflection: There is more beauty and hope in life even at every stage and every age. The Challenge is to find this truth in your life; embrace and cherish it for your very own.

His Eyes are Aglaze

His Eyes are Aglaze,
Hardly can stand
It is heavy
His presence
For all that wait,
Of a kingdom not of this world
Still can attain
Transition, in this composition,
Hope is Aglaze,
Lost from a location you had been
So in the beginning
And So in the end.

When You Cannot Stand: Whether it be from life and its sting, or from the good Lord who has visited you, the great things that were started will still be the great things at the end. Wait on the Lord, He promises there are special rewards. Some we will see on earth, some when we leave here. However priceless are these things for those that wait.

PART IV

Beautiful Butterfly

Oh Beautiful Butterfly
I can see your wings
There are Colors
Spaced so Perfectly
Throughout
These colors shimmer
You absolutely sparkle and shine
You have been through so much
Look how you have come out
You are truly a Beautiful Butterfly
And there is no Doubt
You have come through to the other side.
Where Victory, Courage, Beauty and Might
Are the only way I can describe
Just the Beauty
Arrayed
Through your Entire Flight

Flight Reflections: It is all part of your beautiful plan designed by the Lord. You are beautiful and everything about you does sparkle and shine to include the rough as well as the smooth. The days when everything is bright and those that are less than ideal is in the Lords' sight. Your entire journey is beautiful, and you are beautiful and the Lord loves you just as you are. Can you see the Lord being pleased with you?

Royal Swans

Royal Swans
Floating on the Royal Pond
Glistening and Flowing
All as One
Bring out the Orchestral sound.
As a statement is made
Among Royal Swans who Sway
In and Around the Royal Pond
A girl on the shoulders of her Father Gestures
A little Boy Runs with His sailboat up ahead.
With a gentle Wind and Gentle sway
Swans float amidst a Royal Air
It is quite a Day
As Swans float away and away. .

Reflection on Swans: This poem I wrote and dedicated to the Queen of England in June of 2019. And it is the Lord that I give credit for this. The blessings of the Lord are numerous and illustrious. They shine, they speak out, and it is because of the Lord allowing me, I was given this Honor and Privilege one to write to the Queen and two to dedicate this poem for the Majesty her Queen Elizabeth the 2nd.

Is there something special you would like to achieve while you are going through your life? Perhaps writing a book or a poem or visiting the sick or starting an orphanage, or running a marathon, or hiking a mountain, or ......? What steps are you willing to take, to begin and embrace it as part of your journey of life and keepsake?

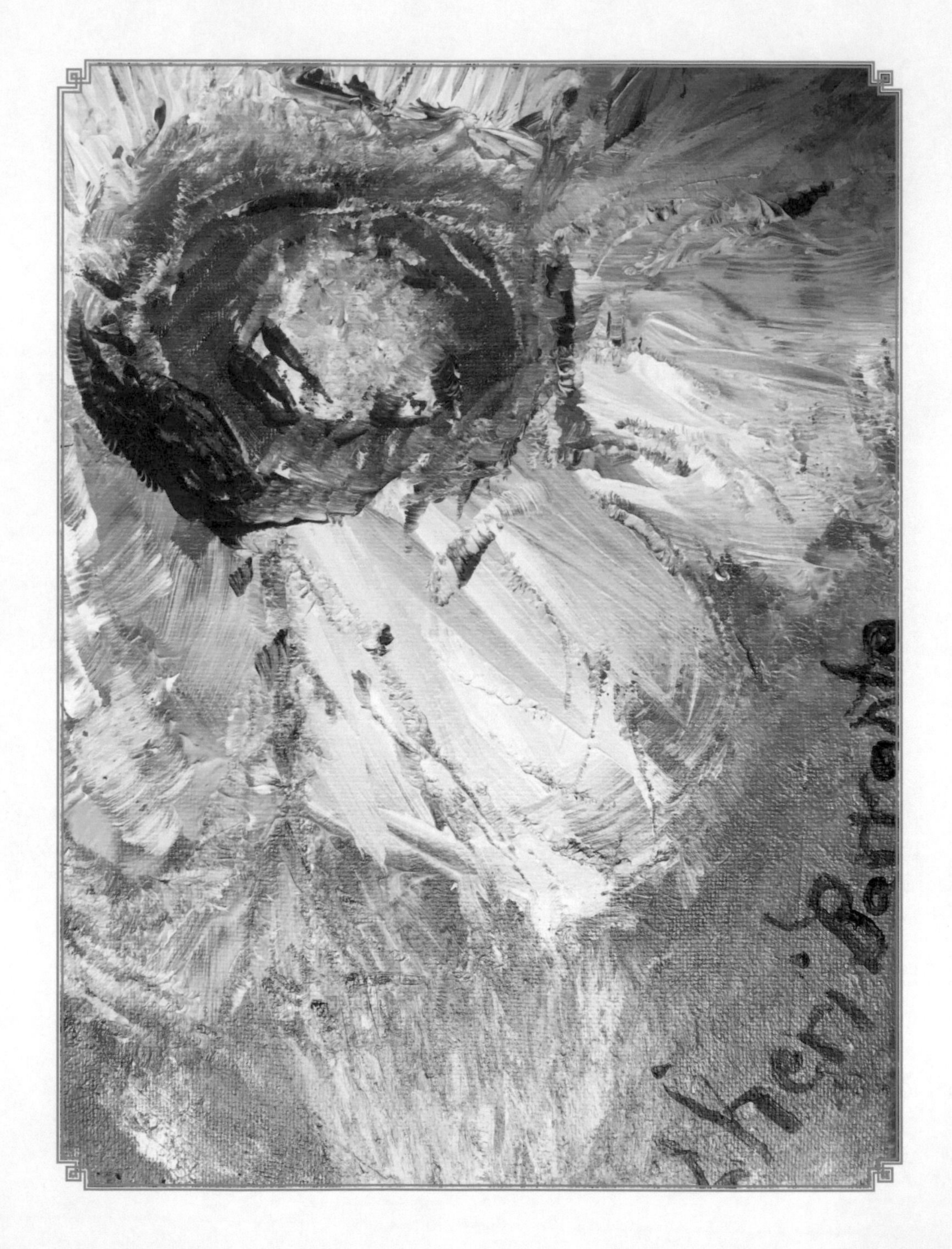

Conclusion

You have your own story. You have a beautiful journey to take. If you are inspired by even a couple of poems for your journey, that sounds great. It was and is and will be my hope and prayer that you will be all the better after reading this book and embracing your best. You are very special and each day you have is a treasure. All the best as you read, think over, and embrace something great in this book.

Printed in the United States
By Bookmasters